Expert Product Management

Advanced Techniques, Tips & Strategies For
Product Management & Product Marketing

By Brian Lawley

D1125556

HappyAbout.info

20660 Stevens Creek Blvd.
Suite 210
Cupertino, CA 95014

Expert Product Management:
Advanced Techniques, Tips & Strategies For Product Management & Product Marketing

First Printing: October, 2007
Paperback ISBN: 1-60005-079-4 (978-1-60005-079-4)
Place of Publication: Silicon Valley, California, USA
Paperback Library of Congress Number: 2007937602

eBook ISBN: 1-60005-080-8 (978-1-60005-080-0)

Trademarks

Warning and Disclaimer

Praise for Expert Product Management

"Being an expert in product management means knowing what is critical for product success. The strategies and tools offered in 'Expert Product Management' will allow new or seasoned practitioners to avoid the non-essential and stay focused on the critical path to plan, build and launch a market-leading product."
Michael J. Salerno, Co-founder and President Emeritus, Boston Product Management Association

"Brian Lawley has done a great job pulling together tangible and practical tools and tips that product managers can immediately put to use to increase the success of their product launches."
Noël Adams, President, PhaseForward and President NorCal PDMA (Product Development and Management Association)

"In technology product management, there are four pragmatic techniques every product manager needs to master. In 'Expert Product Management,' Brian Lawley has written a no-fluff, concisely written guide to these areas. This book contains a lot of information and sound advice that I haven't seen in other product management books, such as its succinct examination of several Road Mapping techniques."
Therese Padilla, Co-founder, AIPMM (Association of International Product Marketing & Management)

"'Expert Product Management' is an excellent guide to managing the more complex, but critical aspects of product management such as roadmapping and product launches. The book provides an invaluable professional validation for experienced product managers and it is a must-have learning tool for new PMs."
Alyssa Dver, CPM, CPMM, Author of "Software Product Management Essentials", PM consultant and teacher

Dedication

This book is dedicated to my wife and family, who have been incredibly patient and understanding in supporting my continued pursuit of Product Management as a career, and to all of those who strive to bring great products to market.

Acknowledgements

I would like to thank the many mentors, bosses, colleagues, acquaintances and product teams that I have had the pleasure of working with and learning from throughout my career. Without them this book would never have been possible.

A Message From Happy About®

Thank you for your purchase of this Happy About book. It is available online at http://happyabout.info/expertproductmanagement.php or at other online and physical bookstores.

- Please contact us for quantity discounts at sales@happyabout.info
- If you want to be informed by e-mail of upcoming Happy About® books, please e-mail bookupdate@happyabout.info

Happy About is interested in you if you are an author who would like to submit a non-fiction book proposal or a corporation that would like to have a book written for you. Please contact us by e-mail editorial@happyabout.info or phone (1-408-257-3000).

Other Happy About books available include:

- Scrappy Project Managment:
  http://happyabout.info/scrappyabout/project-management.php
- 42 Rules of Marketing:
  http://happyabout.info/42rules/marketing.php
- Overcoming Inventoritis:
  http://happyabout.info/overcoming-inventoritis.php
- Foolosophy:
  http://happyabout.info/foolosophy.php
- Tales From the Networking Community
  http://happyabout.info/networking-community.php
- Happy About Online Networking:
  http://happyabout.info/onlinenetworking.php
- Confessions of a Resilient Entrepreneur:
  http://happyabout.info/confessions-entrepreneur.php
- Climbing the Ladder of Business Intelligence
  http://happyabout.info/climbing-ladder.php
- The Business Rule Revolution:
  http://happyabout.info/business-rule-revolution.php
- Happy About Global Software Test Automation:
  http://www.happyabout.info/globalswtestautomation.php
- Happy About Joint Venturing:
  http://happyabout.info/jointventuring.php
- The Home Run Hitter's Guide to Fundraising
  http://happyabout.info/homerun-fundraising.php

Contents

Figures

1 Introduction

There are many books and training courses on the basics of product management and product marketing. These provide an excellent foundation for new product managers, or even for those who have been around a while but want to sharpen their skills and ensure they are using best practices.

This book is designed to go one step beyond the other books and training available today. Its focus is to cover four of the most critical elements in ensuring product success, and to convey practical strategies, insights, tips and techniques that I have learned from hands-on experience defining, launching and marketing over fifty products during the last twenty years of my career. This includes best practices learned from Apple, Symantec, Adobe and dozens of startup and mid-sized firms that my company, the 280 Group, has helped with Product Management and Product Marketing consulting projects.

We'll be covering how to prioritize features and build product roadmaps, which is absolutely critical for getting your team and company on the same page and for delivering the right features in your product at the right time. We'll also cover how to run effective Beta programs, which can oftentimes mean the difference between shipping a poor-quality product and shipping a product that you have a high degree of confidence in. From there we'll talk about how to plan and execute an effective product launch. Short of building a great product, product launches are one of the most (if not THE most) critical factors for achieving success. And finally, we'll discuss how to get phenomenal reviews for your products. Oftentimes this is an area that is an afterthought, and is not dealt with until or unless the product receives poor reviews. With a well-managed review program, you can turn press and analysts into one of your most powerful marketing weapons, further accelerating the success of your product.

In addition to these four areas there are, of course, other key things to focus on to ensure your product's success. We'll be covering these in future books as well as in our monthly newsletter, PM 2.0, which is available on our website.

Though the information in this book is based on experience with high-tech software and hardware products, in many cases it will be highly applicable to all kinds of other products. The fundamentals of good Product Management and Product Marketing remain true across different types of products, though the details of execution may vary.

All of the techniques and information outlined in this book have been used in real-world situations with great success. Virtually all of the documents and tools that are discussed in this book are available on our website (some free, others as part of our toolkit series), giving you the ability to leverage them to get more done, deliver better results and save time.

We hope the information you learn from this book will help you to ship many great new products that delight your customers, change the way they live and work and make significant profits for your company. We wish you success as you go about defining, launching and marketing your new products!

2 Product Roadmaps

Effective product planning can dramatically improve your results and give you a much higher chance of success. It leads to better products, reduced development costs and a much better chance for maximizing revenues. This chapter will discuss how to perform high-level planning in the form of roadmaps, how to prioritize features and how to use different types of organizing strategies to determine what features should be in each release.

Why a Roadmap?

Product Roadmaps can mean the difference between success and failure when delivering and marketing products. They can be one of the most effective tools in a Product Management professional's arsenal. When created and used correctly, they can help win and keep large customers and partners, and can guide the engineering and strategic planning efforts of a company. Unfortunately most Product Roadmaps are created "on the fly" and under pressure when sales or the company management makes a last-minute request. As a result they don't have the impact they should, and can be a source of much trouble if you aren't careful.

As a Product Management professional who is responsible for the overall success of your product, it is important that you create a product roadmap that is compelling, can drive the strategy for your company and development efforts and can provide your partners, press, analysts and customers with a clear idea of where you are headed.

There are many different reasons for developing product roadmaps. It could be that your sales force is losing a large deal and they need to reassure a customer of your future direction. Or it could be that you are briefing the press or analysts and want to reassure them of your company's direction. It might be that you need an internal roadmap to guide engineering efforts and assign resources according to well-thought-out priorities. Or you may need a roadmap to secure your company's next round of funding.

There are wide variations in terms of definitions and uses for roadmaps. The first step is to decide what type you need and what it will be used for.

What is a Product Roadmap?

One of the challenges of creating a roadmap is that there is a very wide variation in terms of definitions and uses. If you look up the definition of "Product Roadmap", you get a very broad range. One definition is "a detailed plan or explanation to guide you in determining a course of action." A second is "a high level sketch of where the company's products are going to give internal and external constituents the ability to plan accordingly."

So what is a Product Roadmap? Is it detailed or is it high level? The answer is that it depends on how you intend to use the roadmap and also whether it is being used internally or outside your company.

Types of Roadmaps

There are lots of different types of roadmaps, and we're going to go through each one. We'll discuss the benefits of each type and how to construct them one by one.

Market and Strategy Roadmap

The first type of roadmap is called a Market and Strategy Roadmap. The idea is to outline exactly which markets you are going to be entering, and then define the strategy you are going to be using to enter them.

Market & Strategy Roadmap

	Year One	Year Two
Markets	Healthcare	Financial Manufacturing
Partner	XYZ Company	
Build In-House		2.X Release
Acquire		Data analytics

Figure 1: Market & Strategy Roadmap

For instance, in this case, in year one, the company is going to be entering the healthcare market. They are going to do it by partnering with XYZ company. Then in year two they'll enter the financial and manufacturing markets by building in-house and acquiring.

This is an excellent way to communicate at a high level which markets you want to go after, what your strategy is and whether you're going to build or buy, acquire technology or use partnerships.

Visionary Roadmap

The next type of roadmap is called the Visionary Roadmap. To create a visionary roadmap, you map out the industry trends on the bottom of the roadmap and then map out your company's high-level vision of the future on the top

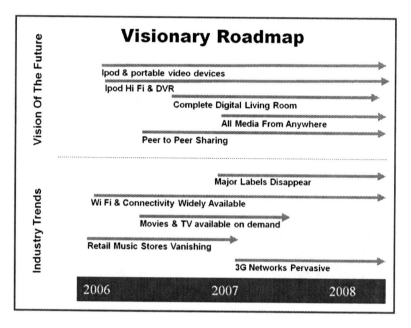

Figure 2: Visionary Roadmap

This is an example of a visionary roadmap that Steve Jobs might have used for Apple's digital media strategy. It shows the underlying events that are happening in the marketplace and then paints a picture of what corresponding products will be delivered to take advantage of the trends. For instance, in the hypothetical example above, as Wi Fi and movies-on-demand become prevalent, Apple indicates a possible focus on delivering a complete digital living room plus the ability to access all your media from anywhere.

Visionary roadmaps are very powerful in terms of painting a big picture and showing that you understand the landscape and are actively exploiting trends.

Technology Roadmap

Another type of roadmap is a Technology Roadmap. The idea behind the Technology Roadmap is to show, on the top level, what the technology advances are that are going on in the industry and then, on the bottom level, to show your actual product plans that are based on those technology advances.

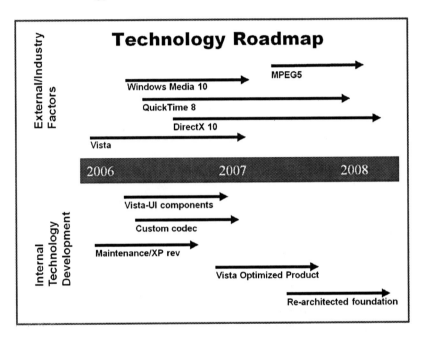

Figure 3: Technology Roadmap

This is a great way to communicate what your dependencies are going to be. It also helps to communicate that your company understands what's happening technologically in the marketplace and how you are going to be taking advantage of it and fully leverage the technologies that are available to you.

Technology Across Products Roadmap

Below is an example of a roadmap of Technology Across Products. The idea here is that if you have shared components, or a new architecture that is going to be used in multiple products you can show on a timeline basis which products will be using which components.

Technology Across Products

	2006	2007	2008
Product 1	Codec		New Architecture
Product 2		Codec Vista UI	
Product 3		Vista UI	New Architecture
Product 4	Codec		New Architecture

Figure 4: Technology Across Products Roadmap

This type of roadmap can be very useful if you have an internal group that you are dependent on that is creating technologies that will be shared across a variety of products.

Platform Roadmap

Another type of roadmap that is commonly used is called a Platform Roadmap. Platform roadmaps are useful if you have a software or hardware platform that other companies build products upon. For example, Microsoft, Palm, Google, Salesforce.com and eBay all have platforms that allow developers to create products that tie into their offerings.

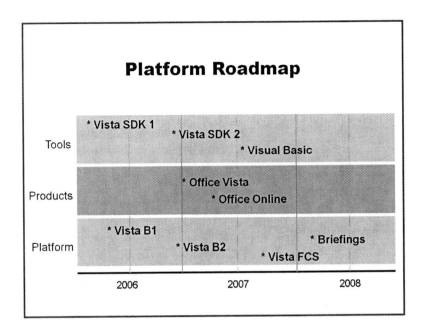

Figure 5: Platform Roadmap

A platform roadmap should include the plans for the platform itself, such as when different versions are coming out and what the overall design and theme for each release is. It should also include information about what development tools will be available for developers to take advantage of new versions of the platform. And finally, it should include any products that will be released by the platform vendor, so that third-party developers will know what to expect and can be reassured that the platform vendor is also investing heavily in the new platform.

Product Roadmap

Now we are going to cover the most common type of roadmap, the Product Roadmap. We'll discuss both internal roadmaps and external roadmaps, and we'll go through an eight-step process for creating them.

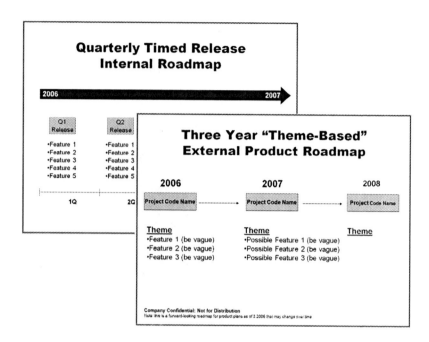

Figure 6: Internal/External Product Roadmaps

Product Roadmaps are used to convey the high-level plans for a product to a variety of audiences. Internal roadmaps are used to help solidify product decisions, guide resource allocation and communicate with other constituents in the company about where the product line is going. External roadmaps are used to convey to customers, press, analysts, partners and others where the company is headed with its products.

Eight-Step Process for Creating a Product Roadmap

The eight-step process gives you a systematic formula for creating a compelling internal product roadmap. Using the internal roadmap as a basis, you can then create an external roadmap for use with partners and others outside your company.

Step 1: Determine the Detail Level & Time to Spend

The first step in the process is to decide how much detail you want to include and how much time you want to spend on preparing the roadmap.

There are several factors to consider: What is the shelf life of the roadmap actually going to be? How important is it going to be to your company? Is it just a loose plan or is it a firm commitment? Is it going to drive the strategy in your company or is it just going to be something that gets used once in order to close a large deal, and isn't mentioned ever again?

Based on how important the roadmap is going to be, you can choose the appropriate method. That method might be just to draw up a quick-and-dirty roadmap - open up a template, put several products on it, send it to your sales team and then you are done.

Alternatively, the roadmap might be something that is more of a mid-level analysis going through something like these full eight steps, where you've really put some good thought into it. In this case it is much more of a strategic tool, and deserves more in-depth thought.

If your company takes product roadmaps very seriously and you have extensive time and resources to spend, you might choose to use one of the software product planning tools available (See the PM Software Comparison in the Resources section of the 280 Group Website at www.280group.com). These tools give you very powerful capabilities to make "what-if" decisions and analyze multiple different scenarios. However, they require substantial financial, time and management commitment in order to be used effectively.

Step 2: Competitive, Market & Technology Trends

The next step is to create a roadmap that shows the competitive, market and technology trends. This is going to be important because, once you have finished your product roadmap, you'll want to come back and compare it to this slide as a reality check from a competitive and market point of view to ensure that your roadmap makes sense.

Figure 7: Competitive, Market & Technology Trends Roadmap

Step3: Gather & Prioritize Requirements

Step three is to gather and prioritize your requirements. Ideally you already have an MRD (Market Requirements Document) and a PRD (Product Requirements Document) for your next release, showing what features you are planning to include. You may also have a list of all of the feature requests that you have gathered for future releases. Add to this list by gathering additional requirements from all the other shareholders such as your sales force, executives, technical support staff, field sales engineers, press, analysts and anyone else who has offered you good ideas. The goal is to capture the full universe of feature possibilities.

After you have a complete list of requests, take the data and put it into a prioritization matrix. The matrix helps you rank the criteria and figure out which features are most important for your upcoming releases.

Prioritization Matrix

0 = low
5 = high

Application/Major Feature/Service	Details	Requestor	User Pain (0 - 5)	Upsell revenue (0 - 5)	New Revenue (0 - 5)	Competitive necessity (0 - 5)	TOTAL SCORE
		Weight	25	25	30	20	Total 100
Launch performance	Launch in <2 seconds	Customers, support	5	3	0	5	3
Auto-entry for signup	Import data from to reduce signup time	Customers	3	2	1	4	2.35
IE 7.0 support	Support for new security features	Customers, Management	4	2	5	5	4

Figure 8: Feature Prioritization Matrix

Figure 8 shows an example of a feature prioritization matrix. You can use it to assign a weight to each different column, and then assign a ranking for each of the features based on the criteria along the top row (use any criteria that you think are appropriate). Once you are done, you can sort by the end column and get a sense of relative importance of all the features against each other, and what the priorities should be for upcoming releases.

Step 4: Decide on Timeframe

Next, decide on a timeframe. Should it be quarterly, or should it be annual? Do you want to show one year, three years, five years or some combination? The answers to these questions are dependent on what the roadmap will be used for. For strategic planning, it is likely to be a three to five-year roadmap. For briefing customers and the press, it may only be for the next four to six quarters.

Step 5: Choose Organizing Strategy

Next, choose an organizing strategy. There are three strategies that you can use:

1. Themes
2. Golden Feature
3. Timed Releases

Theme Strategy

To use the theme strategy, take the prioritization matrix and find logical groupings of high-scoring items. Then assign the groupings a theme name. For example, a logical group might be a theme for performance. Features that would fall under this theme might be launch times, screen refresh, time to update a backend database, etc. Themes can be used for a major release with many features, and they can also be used for bug fixes or a "Cleanup release," particularly for a 0.1 or a 0.01 release.

One great thing about themes is they help resist "feature creep" because, when the team comes to you with an additional feature request, you can look at it and see whether or not it fits into the concept of the theme you have agreed upon. If it doesn't fit with the theme, defer it to a later release.

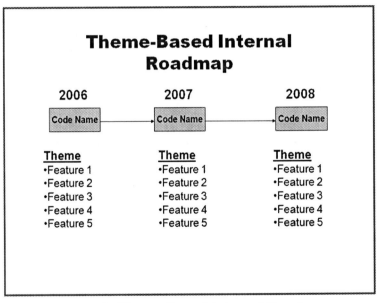

Figure 9: Theme-Based Internal Roadmap

Figure 9 displays an example of an internal theme-based roadmap. At the top are the years and the code names for the products. Below are the themes and then the key features that fit into that theme.

Golden Feature Strategy

To use the Golden Feature technique, choose a single feature that is the absolute most important priority for the release, and then get the entire team to rally around it as the focus. This single feature provides enough customer value on which to base the entire release. It is compelling enough that all of your customers will want to upgrade (and some potential new customers will be further convinced to purchase). And it is simple enough to communicate from a marketing and competitive point of view that it gives your product a noticeable boost.

Ideally the Golden Feature can be described in one to five words. Some examples might include:

1. 30% Faster Performance
2. Import MS Word files or
3. Double your battery life.

It has to be simple and very compelling. If your release has a long list of features, but you can't find a one to five word value message to communicate, it's going to be very hard to build a marketing campaign and keep your product focus.

The Golden Feature technique is particularly effective if you are on short release cycles or are doing a point release (1.1, 1.2, etc). Your team members may want to include all kinds of other features that can be of varying interest and value to your customers. If you can get them focused on the one Golden Feature for the release (and get them to agree that everything else is a "nice to have" priority but that you won't hold up the release for it), you'll have a much better chance of success. You'll also have a higher likelihood of meeting a tight schedule, as you can plan the release with more certainty if the Golden Feature is the only critical path item.

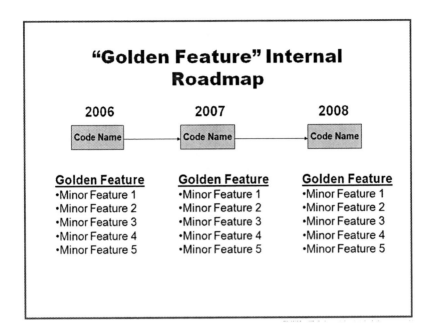

Figure 10: Golden Feature Internal Roadmap

Timed Release Roadmap

The timed release strategy uses pre-determined release dates, rather than features, to drive the schedule. Decide on a release interval (quarterly, every six months, once a year, etc.) and then take the prioritized feature list and estimate which of the top features can make it into each release. If a feature misses the release, it gets moved to the next one.

The timed release strategy has the advantage of providing your customers, partners and internal company constituents with known ship dates they can plan around. It also alleviates the pressure of everyone trying to get their "pet" feature into the next release, since they know that there will be another release coming along shortly. The downside of the timed release strategy is that it doesn't work very well for features that have long development cycles. If your team is working on a feature that will take several release cycles to complete, resources may be diverted to finish work for the interim release and the larger feature may never get completed.

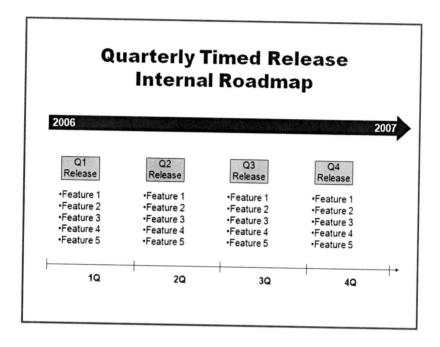

Figure 11: Quarterly Timed Release Internal Roadmap

Figure 11 is an example of a quarterly timed release internal roadmap displaying the four quarterly releases and the key features that are expected to be in each of those releases.

Step 6: Build Internal Roadmap

Now that you have gathered and prioritized all of the features and selected an organizing strategy, the next step is to create a roadmap that conveys the decisions. You can use one of the 280 Group roadmap templates (available in the 280 Group Product Roadmap Toolkit at www.280group.com in the "Products" section) or you can create your own from scratch using PowerPoint or Excel. For the internal roadmap, include as much detail as possible. It needs to convey enough information so that anyone looking at it will immediately gain a quick understanding of what is being worked on (for the external roadmap we'll remove much of this detail).

Step 7: Fine Tune and Get Buy-In

Step seven is to compare your roadmap against the competitive, technology and market trend slide that was created at the beginning of the process. From there review it with internal constituents to explain the reasoning and get buy-in from the stakeholders in your organization.

Ideally, roadmaps should be created in a collaborative way with your team. Don't just show up with something already finalized that your engineers and sales people haven't had a say in and haven't bought into. Get them involved early, show them the process you are using for prioritizing and planning, and they will be more likely to support the final results.

Take the working draft of the roadmap and work with engineering to determine feasibility, do resource load balancing and make sure the schedule is viable. You'll also want to run it by sales so they get a sense what you are thinking; what's coming next, etc., and of course get buy-in from management, support, operations and any other key stakeholders.

Step 8: Create External Roadmap

The final step is to create an external roadmap. To do this use the internal roadmap as the basis and remove features and details so it is appropriate to actually show outside your company.

This is one of the places where themes and golden features can be very useful because you can put a theme on the roadmap without including the underlying details and, depending on the audience, you can choose whether to reveal additional information. For example, if pressed for details you might say "In the next release we're focusing on performance. We've got about a dozen features that fall into that theme, and we'll provide additional details at a later date."

For external roadmaps, make sure to put the appropriate caveats, including that the content is confidential, that plans may change, etc. Also, you may not want to include specific dates on an external roadmap. Oftentimes it is better to be much more generic and vague and just show a map of releases over an undefined time period so you are not committed to specific quarters, years or dates.

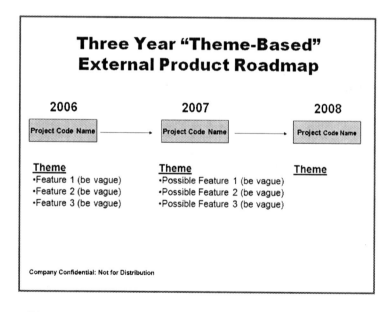

Figure 12: Three Year Theme-Based External Product Roadmap

Chapter 2: Product Roadmaps

Figure 12 is an example of a three-year, theme-based, external product roadmap. For the first year, the name and the features are shown. For the second, the theme is shown and then some possible features. For the third, fourth, fifth, etc., all that is shown is the theme. This allows you to paint a picture of what's coming in the short term, and also to convey to your partners and your customers that you have plans for the future - without having to reveal all the details.

Multiple Product Line Roadmaps

In addition to conveying plans for one product line in your roadmaps, you may want to show multiple product lines. To do this, use the eight-step procedure for each of the product lines, gather information about all the projects and then rank the projects against each other using a prioritization matrix for projects. From there determine where the cutoff line is, based on available resources and priorities of the company. Any time someone proposes a new project where there is a significant change, go back and re-rank the items.

Multiple-Project Prioritization Matrix

0 = low
5 = high

| | | | Weight | | Total points |
| | | | 40 | 60 | 100 |
Project/Release	Details	Requestor	Strategic Importance (0 - 5)	Potential revenue (0 - 5)	TOTAL SCORE
1 Version 8.0 Major Release	Major release. Theme: Performance	PM	2	4	64
2 Custom work for large customer	One-off deal for large customer	Sales	2	5	76
3 Architecture rewrite	Support plug-ins	Eng	4	3	68
4 New ASP-based product	Launching 8.0 as an ASP service	Board	2	3	52
5 New Product Line	Details TBD	Execs	4	1	44
6 Japanese localization release	Full version of 8.0 in Japanese	Japan GM	2	5	76

Figure 13: Multiple Project Prioritization Matrix

To use the prioritization matrix, list each project and then rank projects in terms of strategic importance and revenue potential. Once you are finished, as in the feature prioritization matrix, sort by the end column to get a clear idea of exactly what's most important for your company.

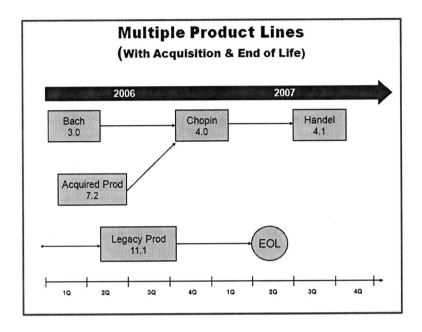

Figure 14: Multiple Product Line Roadmap

Using Multiple Roadmaps Together

You may also want to use a combination of different types of roadmaps together. For example, you may want to create the vision, then show the competitive and technology landscape and then show the actual product roadmap. This gives the product roadmap additional context, helps build a compelling story and conveys that your plan is well thought out.

Roadmap Best Practices

As we said earlier, collaborate early with your team so that they understand the process you are going through and also understand how you derive the results. You may want to have them help you rank the features in the prioritization matrix, so they feel like they've provided some input and understand where the numbers and decisions came from.

Always use code names for projects on your roadmaps. You never know where a roadmap is going to end up and it's much better to have a code name so you haven't committed to a formal name in the market place, and so that competitors will have a more difficult time determining exactly what your roadmap is trying to convey.

Release your roadmaps as uneditable, password-protected Adobe Acrobat PDF files (this requires Acrobat Professional from Adobe). Otherwise, if you deliver them as PowerPoint presentations or in another similar format, inevitably someone will change some of the details. The last thing you want to have happen is for a sales rep or someone else from your company to create their own roadmap and present it to a customer, making commitments for your company that haven't been agreed upon.

Lastly, don't forget international and minor releases in your roadmaps. Include enough detail so that anyone can view the roadmap and very quickly get a snapshot of all the work that is being planned.

3 Beta Programs

After the roadmap and the market and product requirements are delivered to your engineering team, development will begin. When the product is nearing a stable point where all features are implemented, it is time to plan and run a beta program. Beta programs are often overlooked by many companies until it is too late, resulting in shipment of poor quality products, lost sales and sometimes even more significant negative consequences.

Why Beta Programs Are Critical

A well-run beta program can provide you with the external validation you need to ship a product with confidence. It can tell you whether the product is truly going to satisfy customers and meet the quality level you are seeking. It can also provide you with early learning and feedback, customer testimonials and quotes. And finally, it can help you build ongoing relationships with your customers that you can leverage when tough feature decisions come up in the future. A beta program can help to make or break your product's success.

First, a Bad Example

Before we move on to how to succeed in your beta program, I'd like to tell you about a recent experience that I had. I was contacted by a friend who was launching a startup company. He has a very interesting new product, and wanted to know if I would participate in the beta program to make sure it was ready to launch. All I had to do was agree to the terms, download the client software and spend a few hours using the software. To incent me even further, there would be daily contests where I could win gift certificates just for beta testing the software. I was pretty excited, and not only signed up myself but recruited several other people to join in.

When the beta test began, I downloaded the software and installed it. I was ready to spend an hour or two each day for the next few weeks helping out my friend and earning some gift certificates.

Unfortunately I had a very bad experience. I logged on and couldn't figure out how to use the product. There was no documentation or help system and the UI was far from final. I decided to wait until the software was updated so that it wouldn't be a waste of my time.

As the weeks progressed I got emails announcing that new builds were available. However, they never included details about what had been fixed or changed. I reinstalled at one point, only to find that I still couldn't figure out how to use the product. Eventually I lost confidence. I ignored any further emails and never ended up testing out the software. I'm not even sure when the test ended or what the results were. I'm not sure whether the company ultimately ended up shipping a quality product, but I would bet that it was not as good as they wanted it to be.

Now, a Good Example

Now I'd like to tell you about a beta program success story. Years ago, I was Director of Product Management for a startup company named Whistle Communications, which made a product called the InterJet, an Internet appliance for small businesses.

As we approached launch, we were under tremendous pressure. We had to decide when to turn on manufacturing to build the first units, which was a multi-million dollar commitment. We knew that if we made a mistake and began building the product before it was ready, the company would run out of money. We also had a very high-profile PR campaign planned, and we needed customers who were willing to tout the product's virtues.

I launched a beta program that resulted in 10 customers using the product intensively for 10 weeks. Not only did we get confirmation that the product was ready for manufacturing, we were able to test it in a variety of environments not covered in our QA plan, and we got in-depth early feedback for product planning purposes.

The result was that we had a high confidence level that we were ready to ship, had a good idea of what needed to be done next to the product, and had excellent customer references, quotes and success stories prior to our press tour.

How to Run a Beta Program

Running a successful beta program isn't rocket science, but there are several considerations to take into account. The following is a list of factors to keep in mind:

- Setting goals

- Writing the plan & getting sign off

- Deciding who will manage the program

- Determining the length of program

- Recruiting participants

- Selecting candidates

- Defining factors in response rates

- Estimating participation levels

- Obtaining agreements

- Determining incentives

- Starting the program

- Maintaining ongoing communication

- Responding to participants

- Communicating internally

- Administering exit surveys

- Writing a final report

We'll cover each of these topics in more depth in the next few pages.

Beta Program Timeline

To give you an idea for planning purposes of how much time an effective beta program takes, we've put together this rough timeline. The schedule will be highly dependent on what your goals are for the program, but you should plan on 8-12 weeks to run a very comprehensive beta program.

Beta Program Timeline

Task	Amount of Time
Set goals, write plan, sign off	1 week
Recruit & receive applications	3 weeks
Select, notify, send agreement	1 week
Run program	3-6 weeks
Exit survey, tally results, write final report	1 week
TOTAL	8-12 weeks

Figure 15: Beta Program Timeline

Setting Goals

The first step is to determine what your real goals are and get your team and executives in agreement. We suggest that you determine the goals of the beta program as early as possible in the product development process. Ideally you can even mention the goals in the Market Requirements Document (MRD) so that the team has expectations set early on. You'll want to reiterate these goals in a separate beta plan, which we'll cover later. The goals should be as concrete as possible, and you should make sure that your team and executives are in agreement up-front.

Potential Beta Program Goals

There are many reasons to run a beta program. The key is to be clear about what is important. Here are just a few of the goals you may want to include:

- Do you want to validate whether the product is ready to ship?

- Do you want to supplement your QA efforts to cover configurations that aren't being tested in-house?

- Are you looking for early customer references, or do you just want participants to find bugs for you?

- Are you trying to gather feedback to get ahead of the curve for the next version of the product?

- Do you want to make the launch smoother by finding support issues and documenting them in an FAQ?

- Do you intend to support press, analysts and influencers using the product for early reviews during the beta?

Depending on which of these you choose, your strategy for recruiting, qualifying and supporting participants will vary quite a bit.

Examples of Concrete Goals

Here are some examples of concrete goals you might want to consider:

- You might want to test the ship-readiness of the product. To do this you can set metrics around the program such as having at least 20 companies use the product for at least a month. Or you may want to use a qualitative measure such as "The product may not be deemed ready for shipment until ninety percent of the beta customers agree that it is ready to ship."

- You may want to supplement your QA efforts. Looking at your QA test plan, are there any areas that are weak? Are there any customer configurations that are particularly difficult for you to recreate in your testing efforts?

- You may want to set some goals around your launch activities, such as getting at least three companies to be success stories and getting five customer quotes or referenceable customers for the press to contact.

There are almost an infinite number of goals you could choose. The key is to choose the ones that are meaningful based on your project, make them as quantitative as possible, and stick to them.

Beta Program Plan

A beta program plan is critical so that all responsible parties understand and agree up front to their commitments. It needn't be a long document - in fact it is better if it is short, so that there is a higher likelihood that team members will read it. Make sure it includes the key points listed below, and that it is as specific as possible.

- Goals

- Recruiting

- Criteria for starting

- Costs

- Timeline

- Responsibilities

- Criteria for success

- Signoff

Who Manages It?

Who manages your beta program will be a critical decision. Oftentimes it ends up being the Product Manager, Project Manager or QA manager. Many times it is delegated to an Admin or junior person. Or you may choose to bring in a contractor who specializes in beta programs.

The two most important criteria for choosing this person are that they are reliable and that they are able to respond to the customer appropriately. If you have press and analysts in your beta program or customers that are critical accounts for your company, you don't want to put a junior person in charge who doesn't have good people and communications skills to handle difficult questions and issues. Who you choose to be in charge will depend on what your stated goals are. The other critical factor is that the person MUST have enough time to dedicate to doing the job - likely to be at least 10-20 hours per week for the duration of the program. If you assign someone who is overloaded already, your program will suffer.

When Do You Start?

Deciding when to actually start the program and deploy the product should be determined early on in the process. Some possible criteria could be to begin when:

1. There are no crashing bugs
2. The bug count has stabilized
3. The internal team has been using the product successfully for a specified number of weeks

You may choose one or a combination of these. Once that first customer is successfully running and stabilized, then you can deploy more widely, having gotten any issues out of the way.

How Long?

The most common reason that beta programs fail is that the team underestimates the time needed for the program or they decide very late in the process to cut the beta program down significantly. By default it will often end up being assumed that a program be run in two weeks. This is incredibly optimistic, and doesn't take into account the fact that beta users may have other priorities that may deter them from even installing the product for a week or two after they receive it.

On the flip side, a longer program is very difficult to keep going. customer interest in helping you out drops off and the last few weeks become virtually worthless. This is dependent on the type of product you have and the incentives - if it's an exciting product and you have a contest for finding bugs you might be able to sustain a longer beta program

The ideal length for most products is 4-6 weeks. This gives you enough time to ramp up the customers, get good feedback and get some sustained usage. Murphy's Law also applies here - if you plan for 6 weeks you'll likely end up doing a 3-4 week program because inevitably the schedule will slip or other factors will come into play.

Recruiting Participants

There are many different potential sources and approaches for recruiting participants:

- Current customers

- Prospects who didn't purchase

- VCs/Investors

- Personal networks

- Sales force and leads

- Advertisements (Craigslist, local newspaper)

Depending on how many participants you want and how much time you have, you can recruit via email, phone or your website. Much of this will be dependent on what your goals are and what your expected participation levels will be.

Recruiting

When you begin recruiting participants, you'll want to make sure that you have all of the program details in place. Tell them the basics of the program, what you are asking them to do and why it will be worth their time. Also gather the information about their environment so that you can decide whether they qualify to be in the program.

In your communications make sure you convey the benefits of participation very strongly, so you get a high response. You might also want to come up with a clever name. For example, one beta program that my company, the 280 Group ran for a client was called *The Great Bug Hunt Contest*, and we had a large number of people apply.

Factors in Responses

So what kind of response can you expect? There are a variety of factors that will influence this:

- How popular is your product?

- Are you completely new or unproven?

- Will it require testers to risk interrupting their business?

- Are you an established company, or one they have never heard of?

- Is your marketing pitch compelling, and will you deliver it in a personal way rather than simply as a mass email blast?

For example, if you have a wildly popular and proven product like the Apple iPod, which is from a well-known company and comes with very little risk, you will likely be able to recruit many willing participants. On the other hand, if you have an enterprise software product from an unknown startup that requires test participants to install it in their day-to-day infrastructure and risk crashing, you may not be able to find more than one or two participants.

Incentives

If the factors in getting a good response are working against you, then you should probably provide incentives. For some participants, simply improving the product will be enough. For others, offer a free or reduced price copy of the final product. Or you may want to run a contest, though you need to be careful regarding contest rules in the states in which you do business.

Participation Levels

Figure 16 gives you an idea of how many participants you might expect based on whether the product is brand-new or an existing, well-known product and what kind of recruiting approach you use. One important thing to note is that the percentage of active users is always much smaller than the number that signs up and commits to be part of the program, so always shoot for having a large number of signups.

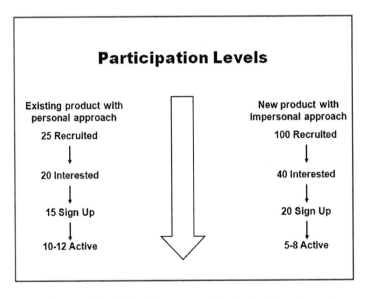

Figure 16: Beta Program Participation Levels

Selection of Candidates

As customers respond indicating they wish to participate in the beta program, capture their details in a recruiting database. Once you have the recruiting database populated with enough responses, you can choose your candidates. Make sure they represent your target customer. Pay particular attention to getting some lower and mid-level users in the mix so that your feature requests and data aren't skewed towards power users (who are usually the ones most likely to participate in beta programs). And finally, make sure the mix supplements your existing QA efforts.

Agreements

Always use beta program agreements because it helps to weed out the participants that aren't serious up-front. A good agreement sets expectations on both sides and includes an NDA (Non-Disclosure Agreement). It doesn't need to be complicated, but it should include the program length, incentives, what you expect them to do and what support you will provide.

For the participants you have chosen, send out the beta agreement and give them a hard deadline to return the materials. Once the deadline passes, you'll then be able to evaluate whether you have a large enough and diverse enough pool of participants to accomplish your goals.

Kicking Off the Program

When you are ready to start the beta program, make sure that you do everything possible to avoid a false start. Double-check the installer and software download sites. Make sure the interface and documentation are ready for customers to use in a meaningful way. And build a FAQ that you can include to help customers from hitting bumps in the road.

Nothing will stall the participation of your beta testers more than having them sit down to get started and then get frustrated if things don't work right. If you don't give them confidence in your product early on, they will be far more likely to drop out of the beta program.

Ongoing Communication

As the program progresses, make sure that you keep the communication going. Use the phone or email to provide participants with status updates from your side and to check in on whether they are staying on top of their commitments to install and use the product. This will give them an increased sense of confidence that it is worth their time to continue using the product.

You'll want to include the following in your communications:

- Start date

- End date

- How to submit bugs/feedback

- Ongoing status

- New build/installation info

- Contest details/additional incentives

Responding To Participants

In your beta agreement and ongoing communications, set an expectation for what kind of response time participants will receive if they encounter problems or have questions. Also, when they submit bug reports or feature requests, acknowledge that you have received them so that they know you are listening.

You can capture information through the Web and into a database, or use email. Email is likely to be much easier and faster and give you a better response, since the participants don't have to log in with a username and password, etc.

Communicating Internally

As the program progresses, make sure you send weekly status reports to everyone involved inside your company. This will add credibility to the program and will decrease the number of people who contact you to ask where the program stands. Include the number of bugs, their priorities and whether the program is meeting the stated goals. Also include the feature requests coming from customers so that the team can see them firsthand.

Exit Surveys

Always end your beta programs with a short exit survey, and make sure that participants MUST fill it out to get any of the incentives. Ask them how much they used the product, their overall impressions, whether they believe it is ready to ship, etc. Also ask them to rank the features in terms of importance and what other suggestions they have for improvement.

You can conduct the survey through email or you can use Zoomerang, Survey Monkey or one of the other online tools. You may also want to visit a few of the most important customers to get more in-depth answers.

Beta Program Exit Survey

1.) What types of tasks did you attempt with the product?

2.) Were you able to save time as a result of using the product?

3.) What did you like best about using the product?

4.) What did you like least about using the product?

5.) Was there anything that confused you about using the product?

6.) Do you believe that the product is ready to ship?

7.) What are the 3 highest priority things that need to be changed?

8.) Rank the value of each of the following features:

1= not compelling
5= very compelling

1.) Feature #1
1   2   3   4   5

2.) Feature #2
1   2   3   4   5

Figure 17: Beta Program Exit Survey

Final Report

As you prepare to ship the product, deliver a final report with recommendations. Include the bug trend info to show that bugs have stabilized, as well as any open issues that customers brought up that aren't resolved. State whether you met the overall goals, and include a summary of customer opinions and feedback from the final survey.

Deliver this report to the team prior to the sign off on the Golden Master or First Customer Ship decision - it will help immensely in making sure that everyone who is signing off has a realistic picture of whether the product is ready to ship.

Follow Up

You've spent a lot of time recruiting the program participants, so don't let your hard work go to waste. At a minimum consider sending "Thank You" letters to them, and you might even want to send them a nice gift so that they are more inclined to participate in your next beta program. Also, leverage the relationships you've started to build. You can ask beta customers if they are willing to be on a customer council or participate in other beta programs in the future. And finally, ask them if you may call them in the future if there are specific features your team wants advice on. Having a few customers you can quickly call to get opinions can be invaluable when your team isn't sure about how to implement a feature or what might be important from a customer point of view.

Best Practices

Make sure to circle back and circulate a brief summary to the team about the program, including what worked and what didn't. This will help your company get increasingly better with each beta program you run. Also, make sure to give thanks and praise to each of your team members - it takes a lot of hard work to execute a beta program.

4 Product Launches

At this point in the product lifecycle, your product is nearing completion. Beta testing is wrapping up, the product is looking good and it is time to turn attention towards bringing the product to market and making the best possible impression. By now you have most likely invested a significant amount of time, money and energy to develop the product. You have carefully defined the feature set, made difficult tradeoff decisions, run a beta program and invested in quality assurance efforts to ensure the product is going to deliver what it promises.

The next step is to launch the product correctly to ensure it has the greatest chance for success. A well-executed launch can mean the difference between success and failure for your product. If you do it right it can give you substantial initial revenue momentum and set your product up to beat its competitors. And it can also give you the ability to get quick feedback and make course corrections if necessary.

Launch Goals

As you are planning your launch, it is important to determine what your goals are up front. This will determine what kind of tactics and programs you want to use, what your budget should be and how much time and effort you'll want to spend on the launch.

There are several things to consider as you set your goals, such as how many leads to generate, revenue to achieve, how strongly to set the competitive argument, how much initial awareness to generate and how many units to get into customers' and channels' hands. It's important to make the goals as specific as possible, because once you have developed your launch plan you'll want to come back to the goals and do a reality check about whether your tactics and budget will be able to achieve what you want.

Types of Launches

There are three types of launches that we are going to be discussing - soft launches, minimal launches and full-scale launches. One of the biggest mistakes that my company, the 280 Group, sees in our consulting engagements is that oftentimes the client's goals require a full-scale launch and budget, but their plans end up being more of a soft or minimal launch and there is a disconnect that has little chance of achieving the goals.

Soft Launch

The first type of launch is a soft launch. Oftentimes companies will do this type of launch if their product isn't fully ready yet and they want to deploy to a limited set of customers. Startups often do this because they do not have the financial and marketing resources to do much more. They may have a need to get the product out quickly, capture some customers and revenues and then use results to go to venture capitalists for additional funding to expand their sales and marketing efforts.

The other reason for doing a soft launch is that a company may want to get the product into customers' hands rapidly to get some quick feedback and iterate the product. For products that are a brand new type of offering, this type of early feedback may be necessary in order to make course corrections to get to a version 2.0 or 3.0 that truly meets market needs.

The downside to a soft launch is that more often than not they generate little or no revenue. Because a soft launch doesn't have the momentum of a big push behind it with the corresponding marketing and PR activities, the launch will oftentimes create little or no press coverage, and the company will find themselves weeks later wondering why they were unable to generate more interest in their product and why they missed their revenue targets.

The biggest downside is that the company may have lost the ability to create excitement and may not be able to recover. Once the "cat is out of the bag" the press may not be interested in covering the product or reviewing it because it is old news. And the coverage that the company does get isn't coordinated so that customers also see their marketing and hear about their product through other channels at the same time as the press coverage. The result is that the company may have to spend significantly more on marketing later to recover.

Of course there are some exceptions to this. Companies founded by well-known people, with incredibly viral product capabilities or with highly contentious products may be able to get away with this. But you have to be realistic - chances are your company will not enjoy this kind of success.

Minimal Launch

A minimal launch is something you want to consider when your funding and resources are limited. You might have a product that isn't that important to your company's strategy and overall success. Or you might be coming up with a minor revision and only wish to make your installed base aware so that they upgrade.

It's also common for companies to fail to plan early enough, and then have to scramble and do a minimal launch because they ran out of time. Or a company may accidentally have a minimal launch (thinking it will meet their goals) because of unrealistic expectations about how important their product is to the market and the assumption that "it will sell itself."

Minimal launches can be very effective if you use your resources wisely. For example, instead of trying to do a horizontal launch to make the entire industry aware of the product, a company may want to target a specific vertical with a combination of direct mail, PR and seminars. If the product is a good solution in that vertical, it may provide the company with the revenues necessary to expand their marketing campaigns on an ongoing basis.

It's important to note that minimal launches can have the same downsides as soft launches. Once a company has launched, they may never be able to recover or may have to spend an extraordinary amount of money to build the revenue momentum that they need.

Full-Scale Launch

A full-scale launch is designed to maximize awareness, generate as many leads and sales as possible, and let the industry know who your company is and why you matter. Even though you are spending more money on a full-scale launch, each dollar is much more effective because your marketing programs build on each other and provide synergy. For example, imagine that you receive dozens of product announcements in publications, followed by advertising that reaches the same readers, followed by excellent product reviews, after which your target customers receive a direct mail piece from you. Each one of these exposures to the potential customer creates additional awareness and credibility and builds on the others, ultimately incenting your prospects to act and buy your product.

Full-scale launches can be broadly horizontal in nature or can target one or multiple verticals (depending on your product and chosen marketing strategy).

A full-scale launch gives your product the best chance of success, though most companies are afraid to spend the money to execute one. Even though they may have spent millions of dollars developing a product that is going to change their customers' lives, when it comes down to spending a few hundred thousand dollars they aren't realistic that this may be required to generate the millions in revenue their plans call for.

Launch Strategy

An excellent strategy for planning is to use a full-scale launch as the starting point. If you are budget, resource or time-constrained, then scale back the plan and use a subset of the programs. This gives you the best chance of success, ensures you don't forget to consider all of the options and allows you to make educated tradeoffs about how you are going to reach your goals.

Elements of a Successful Launch

The elements of a successful product launch are:

- Planning

- Communication

- Timing

- Effective Marketing Mix

- Compelling Messaging

- Budget to Achieve Goals

- Message Reaches Target Customers

- Product Readiness

Making a mistake on any one of these elements can turn your product launch into a failure.

Planning

In terms of planning, it is important to write a product launch plan to pull together your thinking and get consensus on what activities will be occurring.

A typical product launch plan will include the following components:

- Summary

- Purpose of this Plan

- Market Overview

- Key Market Trends

- Target Customers and Their Needs

- Product

- Ship Date/Window of Opportunity

- Positioning

- Tag Line

- Features and Benefits

- Price

- Place and Channel

- Marketing Strategy

- Marketing Tactics/Promotion

- Launch Budget

- Marketing Mix

- Expected ROI

- Action Plan/Deliverable Ownership

- Rough Timeline/Schedule

- Key Decisions Remaining

Communication

Great communication, both internally and externally, is also one of the keys to a successful launch.

Internally at your company, you'll want to form a launch team and have weekly meetings to track deliverables, clarify blocking issues and assign responsibilities and action items. You'll want to communicate the top-level details of the meeting to the stakeholder executives in your company. It is important for them to understand what you are trying to accomplish and who you are relying on in order to be successful.

External communication is also critical. If you launch a new product without allowing your channel or customers enough warning to get ready for it, you may stall product sales. Likewise if you launch a product without pre-briefing analysts and the press (under NDA, of course) they may be blindsided and not express complimentary opinions about your product.

One particularly effective technique for communicating your launch plans, especially at a large company, is to create a one page product overview with all of the critical details included.

Product Name One Page Overview
Company Confidential

100 Word Product Description:

Target Customer(s):

Positioning:

Tag Line:

Top 3 features:

Unique Selling Proposition:

Pricing:

Availability:

Channels Being Used:

Promotions:

Estimated Availability:
Beta version:_____ Golden
Master/FCS/Production/General Availability: _____

Competition:
1.
2.
3.

Top 3 FAQs:
1.
2.
3.

Figure 18: One Page Product Overview

Create this document three to four months prior to launching your product. It will come in extremely handy; whenever anyone emails or calls you to find out about the product and launch details you can send them this document and they will have most of the detail they need without your having to constantly repeat the information.

Chapter 4: Product Launches

Timing

Timing is also critical for a product launch. Ideally you want to have your marketing and PR hit shortly after the product becomes available for customers to purchase. Following this, there should be enough continued marketing and product reviews to keep the sales momentum going.

The easiest way to achieve this is to set a goal based on your estimated ship date and then work backwards. Start planning four months prior to the launch - this will be enough time to plan and execute all PR and marketing activities in order to have them hit just after product availability.

One thing you want to avoid if at all possible is to announce too early. There is always the temptation to do this based on competitive pressure and/or wanting the world to know about the great new product you are working on. The problem is that if you announce too early customers may either purchase a competitor's product because yours isn't available yet or they may learn about your product and never come back again to actually purchase it.

Effective Marketing Mix

The next critical factor for success is choosing what the mix of marketing components is going to be in order for the messages to reach your target audience. One of the big mistakes that companies make is assuming that they only need to do one or two types of marketing in order to get critical mass going. For instance, they may focus on PR activities to get press coverage of the initial product announcement and a few product reviews. Or they may assume that they can focus on bloggers or online forums and quickly get a buzz going for the product. Yet without additional programs such as email campaigns, a trade show or two, webinars, etc. they may never bring in enough leads to have a chance of meeting their sales numbers.

Marketing Mix Components

- PR activities
- Advertising
- Direct mail
- Email campaigns
- Website
- Viral/Guerrilla Marketing

- Channel programs
- Promotions
- Collateral
- Trade Shows
- Launch Event
- Webinars/Seminars

Figure 19: Marketing Mix Components

Ideally there should a mixture of marketing programs and components that will reach the target customers in several ways, building awareness and interest, creating a desire to buy the product and then incenting prospects to take action.

An effective marketing mix will reach the target customer in a synergistic fashion. For example, the potential customer will read a product announcement when it first becomes available. They may then see advertising or receive a direct mail or email piece from you reinforcing your messages. Or they may see email threads going around in online forums they participate in. And then they may see two or three positive product reviews that recommend your product.

The key is to make sure that your activities achieve enough critical mass to be "Above the Bar" in terms of meeting your goals, while at the same time providing an effective return on your investment. Ideally these are a combination of awareness generation tactics such as advertising, PR and online activities combined with demand generation such as direct mail pieces with a call to action. Add to this effective selling tools and a good process for converting your leads to sales and you have a winning combination.

Compelling Messaging

The next critical factor in launching a product successfully is to ensure you have compelling messaging that speaks directly to your audience's pain points and needs. Developing messaging consists of three parts:

1. Developing the positioning,
2. Writing features & benefits and
3. Determining the unique selling proposition.

If it is at all possible, you'll want to test the messaging with your target customers, either through one-on-one interviews, focus groups or online surveys. If you are going to be spending a large amount of money on your product launch, it makes sense to spend $25K for a few focus groups to validate that your messages hit the mark. Plus you can use the focus groups to do a reality check on your pricing and other critical parts of the product mix.

Positioning Strategies

There are several different strategies that can be used for positioning products. You can focus on specific features that the product offers, or on benefits it offers, needs it fulfills or solutions it provides to problems. For example, for specific features you might position your product as "providing XYZ, which no other product in the marketplace offers." In terms of benefits you might say something like "the only product that gives you full performance without the need to perform any maintenance at all, saving you time and hassles."

You can also position for specific usage occasions, such as "the best product for when you are traveling away from the office," by user category, such as "the optimal solution for consultants who work from their home offices" or directly against another product or products using XY charts and matrices.

Positioning Process

The process for developing positioning begins with coming up with several potential ideas for how your product is differentiated in the market. These could be based on specific features, target market segments or any of the strategies just mentioned. Once you have two or three ideas, test them with at least a few customers and with your channel partners to do a reality check. From there you can create matrices and a formal positioning statement from which all of your other messaging such as tagline product descriptions and features and benefits will be based.

XY Axis Positioning Chart

The easiest way to get started doing positioning work is to create an XY chart and map out your position versus your competitors. To do this first make a list of all of the possible advantages and differentiators you believe your product has. These could include performance, total cost of ownership, number of features, support, company stability, time to implement, work or cost required to maintain the solution, or virtually any other advantage you can think of.

Next you want to create several blank XY charts like the one below. Try out several X and Y axis combinations and map out your competitors. Usually within a short period of time a pattern emerges showing your best chance for strongly conveying your advantages. The goal of this exercise is to create, in one simple slide, a picture that tells your whole story in a way that is as memorable and compelling as possible.

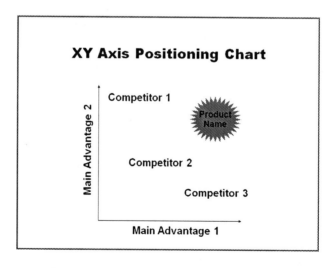

Figure 20: XY Axis Positioning Chart

Matrix Positioning Chart

Another kind of positioning chart is a matrix with four different quadrants. You create a matrix in the same way as the XY chart, mapping your competitors onto the chart and again clearly showing your solution's superiority and advantages over your competitors.

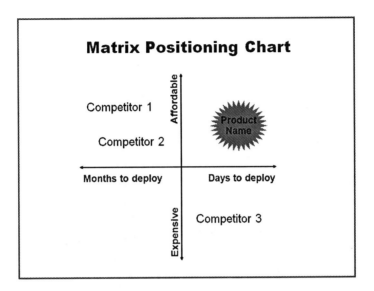

Figure 21: Matrix Positioning Chart

Positioning Statement

Once you have created the XY chart or matrix, you can then fill in a standard positioning statement. The positioning statement sums up the most critical points - who your target customer is, what their need is and what features you provide to solve their problems. It also then specifically calls out why you are better than your competitors.

```
+-------------------------------------------------------+
|                                                       |
|          Positioning Statement                        |
|                                                       |
|                                                       |
|    For [target customers] who need to [primary        |
|    need], [product name] is a [product category]      |
|    that provides [feature 1], [feature 2] and         |
|    [feature 3].                                        |
|                                                       |
|    Unlike [main competitor], [product name]           |
|    delivers [main advantage 1] and [main              |
|    advantage 2].                                       |
|                                                       |
|                                                       |
+-------------------------------------------------------+
```

Figure 22: Positioning Statement

A great positioning statement will instantly get across your message. Virtually anyone else should be able to read it, immediately understand your product's advantage and easily repeat it to others.

One thing to note - don't confuse a tag line and a positioning statement. The positioning statement is meant primarily for your company and its partners whereas the tag line should be meaningful to a wider audience. The tag line is a brilliantly-succinct version of the positioning statement. For example, when I was Product Manager for TrueType font technology at Apple Computer the positioning statement was this:

"For all Macintosh users who need to have crisp and clear fonts at all times, TrueType is a font rendering technology that provides smooth fonts onscreen, great printouts and built-in operating system support."

The tag line for TrueType was: "Great Type, Anywhere, With Ease." It was a derivative of the positioning statement, but was much shorter and more memorable.

Messages, Features & Benefits, USP

Once you have determined the positioning, you can create the rest of the messages that follow. Write short and long descriptions (25, 50, 100 and 250 words) that can be used for the variety of places you'll need them, such as data sheets, websites, online advertising and direct mail and email pieces.

Next write your features and benefits. A common mistake that is often made is that companies communicate about features rather then telling customers why they should care (i.e. the benefit to them). For example, if a company told you that you should buy their product because it uses an embedded Linux operating system it wouldn't necessarily mean much to you. But if they told you they their product includes an embedded Linux operating system which means that you get rock-solid security for your network and corresponding peace of mind then they are telling you why it actually matters to you and what the benefit is.

The key to writing features and benefits is to use the phrase "Which means that you can" as a connector in your sentence. First write the feature, then add "which means that you can" and then fill in the logical answer, which is the corresponding benefit.

The other mistake that companies make is trying to include too many features and benefits because they want to tell you about every single bell and whistle in their product. Don't fall into this trap. If you take all of your top features and prioritize them, then usually, around the fifth feature, the value to the customer starts to decline pretty rapidly.

USP: Unique Selling Proposition

The final thing to create is your Unique Selling Proposition. Simply stated, the USP is a one sentence summary of why the customer should not even consider purchasing anyone else's product. It has to convey the essence of your message, is ideally memorable and easily repeatable and should support the positioning and tag line.

Here is an example of a USP from a product named the InterJet that I worked on at Whistle Communications (acquired by IBM):

"Get your entire small business on the internet securely with web access, email and a website in less than fifteen minutes for under $2,000."

Budget to Achieve Goals

Budgets for product launches vary widely, and are highly dependent on the type of launch you are executing and what your goals are. They can range from $10k for a soft launch to $50k for a minimal launch up to millions of dollars for a large-scale industry launch. The key is to make sure that the amount you spend will allow you to meet the goals you have set out for the launch. If you are a new or unknown company, don't expect to sell $10M worth of new equipment if you are only going to spend $50k to get the word out - it's just not realistic.

One good rule of thumb to use is to look at the financial reports of similar companies in your industry to get an idea of what percentage of their revenues they spend on marketing. This will generally be five to twenty five percent of the expected revenue they generate. If you aren't well-known and are launching a new product you may even want to increase this percentage for your launch as the numbers in annual reports reflect more of the marketing spending amounts for established products already being sold.

Soft Launch Sample Budget

As we outlined earlier, there are many reasons a company may need or want to do a "soft" launch, including lack of budget, product uncertainty and attempting to get revenue traction so they can look for venture capital funding and others.

A typical soft launch budget would look something like this:

- Collateral: $5k

- Adwords Campaign: $4k

- Press release via PR Newswire: $1k

- Guerrilla activities via in-house staff

- Total: $10k

This would be a pretty nominal $10k launch, and would likely also be supplemented by guerrilla activities by in-house staff such as calling the press to attempt to get coverage, placing messages in online forums and other activities.

Minimal Launch Sample Budget

A step up from the soft launch would be to do a minimal launch, including additional elements over and above the soft launch:

- Collateral & Demo: $10k

- Adwords Campaign: $4k

- Press release via PR Newswire: $1k

- Email Blast via purchased list: $10k

- Channel marketing program: $25k

- Guerrilla activities via in-house staff

- Total: $50k

Total cost for a launch like this would be $50k. Again, at this funding and activity level make sure you set your revenue targets and forecasts accordingly.

Full Scale Launch Sample Budget

A full-scale launch would include hiring a PR firm for six months to get you introductions and extensive coverage of both the product announcement and product reviews. It would also include online AdWords advertising, print advertising, extensive collateral and a self-running demo, possibly a trade show and/or launch event, email blasts and channel marketing programs. Total cost for a launch like this could be anywhere from $100k up to several million dollars, although the example here is about $500k.

- PR Firm for six months: $120k

- Adwords Campaign: $5k

- Print Advertising: $250k

- Collateral & Demo: $25k

- Trade Show/Launch Event: $30k

- Email blasts to purchased lists: $20k

- Channel marketing program: $50k

- Total Cost: $500k+

This would give you extensive awareness and the ability for target customers to hear your messages multiple times to get them to act on finding out more and purchasing your product.

Message Reaches Target Customers

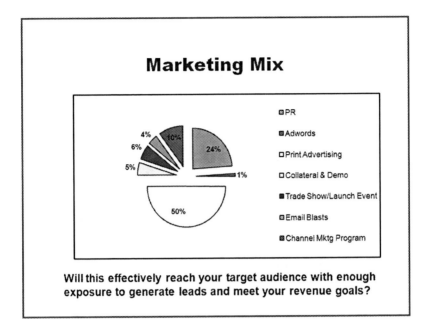

Figure 23: Marketing Mix

Marketing Mix

The marketing mix you choose is also critical. How much are you spending on each of the different components? How effective will each program be? And most importantly, will the mix effectively reach your target audience? The estimate you need to make is whether the mix and overall activities will generate enough exposure to generate a large enough number of leads and sales to meet your revenue goals.

ROI (Return on Investment) Calculation

One way to check your assumptions about the marketing mix is to use an ROI calculation spreadsheet. To do this, first make assumptions about how much profit you'll make per sale. Then estimate the number of exposures to customers you'll get from each program, the percent of these that will become leads and the percent for which you will close the sale. This allows you to build a rough analysis of how much profit you think you can make based on your marketing spending.

ROI Assumptions

ROI Calculations for $500k full-scale launch	
ASSUMPTIONS	
Profit/unit sold	$ 400.00
PR program	
# expected announcements & reviews	10
Average readership of target publication(s)	50,000
% leads from exposures	0.50%
Close rate	20.00%
Adwords/Online Advertising	
Cost per click	$ 0.50
Close rate	2.50%
Print Advertising	
# publications ads will be run in	3
Readership per publication	50,000
# times ad will run	3
% that turn into leads	0.50%
Close rate	0.2
Trade Show/Demo	
# attendees	40000
% that visit booth	3%
% of visitors that turn into leads	40%
Close rate	40%
Email Blasts	
# emails sent to all lists	100,000
% that visit website	1%
Close rate	40%
Channel Marketing Program	
# leads generated	1000
Close rate	40%

Figure 24: ROI Calculation

Using the spreadsheet shown above, you can then estimate the resulting ROI, including the total number of exposures you expect to receive, number of leads, number of sales and corresponding profit.

ROI Results

Program	Cost	# exposures	# leads	# sales	profit
PR program	120,000	500,000	2,500	500	$200,000
Adwords/Online Advertising	5,000	N/A	10,000	250	$100,000
Print Advertising	250,000	450,000	2,250	450	$180,000
Collateral & Demo	25,000	-	-	-	$ -
Trade Show/Launch Event	30,000	1,200	480	192	$ 76,800
Email Blasts	20,000	100,000	1,000	400	$160,000
Channel Mktg Program	50,000	N/A	1,000	400	$160,000
TOTAL	500,000	1,051,200	17,230	2,192	$876,800

Total Profit	$ 876,800
Less total cost	$ (500,000)
Net Return	$ 376,800

ROI	75%

Figure 25: ROI Results

Doing a calculation like this is important because, as you seek approval for your launch plan, it will help you to justify the budget more easily. You can also use this to plug in the results from a soft, minimal and full launch and set expectations about what results will be achieved accordingly.

Product Readiness

Launch Readiness Checklist

Task	Owner	Due Date	Status
Documentation			
Help System			
Packaging			
Support policies			
Add'l support programs			
Support training			
Sales tools & training			
Operations readiness			
Channel training			
Press tour materials			
Collateral			
Beta program completed			
QA completed			
Signoff by executives			
Customer references			
Warranty & return policy			
Website updated			
BOM completed			
Contracts/Legal work			
Marketing plan signed off			
Marketing programs			
International readiness			
Certifications completed			
Promotions in place			
Positioning, tagline, USP			
Pricing signed off			
Sustaining mktg plan			
Forecast signed off			

Figure 26: Product Readiness

The last critical factor in product launch success is making sure that all aspects of the product are ready. This includes sales, manufacturing, operations, channels, customer support, the product quality and associated necessary components. One way to ensure this is to use a launch readiness checklist and track each component in your weekly launch team meetings. This keeps track of who owns what and allows you to make sure everything is on track to be in place for the launch.

5 Review Programs

You've shipped an excellent, market-driven product. You pulled off a first-rate beta program to make sure the product was solid and ready to go. You have early customer feedback and testimonials. And you've run a high-impact product launch to get the word out and get sales and revenue momentum going. Now it's time to follow up and run a review program to make sure your product gets the most additional benefit possible from all of your hard work.

It's important to mention that no matter how good you are at running product review programs, there is tremendous value bringing in a first rate PR (Public Relations) firm in conjunction with your efforts. PR firms will be able to get you introductions to prominent publications and boost your initial credibility. Some PR firms are also very good at adding value over and above the introductions by helping you with messaging and managing the reviewers you are working with. At a minimum, if you have a really good PR firm, it will help you get the introductions and credibility that get the door open so you have a chance of getting into the right publications and talking to the right people.

It is also important to note that without a really good product review program, everything else you do in terms of marketing may be a waste of time. If you run a half million dollar advertising campaign and try to take the market by storm with a variety of marketing vehicles and then negative product reviews appear it won't matter how much time, effort and money you have spent marketing the product.

Why Reviews Are Critical

Reviews establish credibility and are much more believable than your own marketing. Third-party opinions always carry much more weight than what a company says about its own products. Multiple good reviews have the ability to influence the market, create sales momentum and drive your product's brand. And of course, good reviews also lead to winning awards for your products, which give you further visibility.

Good Reviews versus Bad Reviews

What's the difference between a bad review and a good review? The first thing you have to realize is that some products will never win. You'll never get a good review because they are poor products. If you are in charge of a product like this you probably already have a sense of it, and data from your beta programs and other customer feedback will confirm this. In this case you may need to run a review program just to do damage control while your team improves the product for its next version.

On the flip side, many categories of products have a number of participants whose products are equal. The company that has a strong reviewer's program and applies the right tactics often can create the perception that its product is superior and is the leader.

Occasionally there are products that will win no matter what - these are the lucky ones. Even without a good review program, they will get glowing reviews. But if you put in the extra effort to run a first-rate review program, the results can be phenomenal.

Regardless of how good your product is (or isn't), the key is that perception is everything. If you load the argument and do the right thing to make it easy for the reviewer, you are going to create the perception that your product is the best. You can and must manage that perception.

A Day in the Life of a Reviewer

Reviewers are often overworked and underpaid. Some of them are lazy (though most of them are not). Most reviewers have very hectic lives and work schedules just like you and I.

Reviewing products is a lot of work. Product Reviewers are constantly trying out new products. During the course of the reviews many things can go wrong. They may get interrupted, a new product might arrive but they don't really understand exactly what it is, they might be assigned to cover a product that is not in an area they are familiar with or they might try to set up a product and find out that the company forgot to include a license key or the installation or testing doesn't run quite smoothly.

If the reviewer has a problem, they may send an email or make a phone call to the company. Oftentimes the company won't return the call promptly, so they have to go move onto the next product they are reviewing until they get a response and an answer to their question. When they finally receive the information they need they can go back and begin working on the review again.

Add to all of this the fact that reviewers are facing deadlines and have many conflicting priorities and other duties and you can see why it is important to make it as easy as possible for them. Taking this into account, we will now cover the top 10 things you can do to make it much easier for them to be more prone to give you a great review.

#1: Put a Dedicated Senior Product Manager on the Job

The tendency of many companies is to put a junior person in charge of the review program. This can be a fatal mistake, because if something goes wrong or a tough question comes up the person may not know how to respond appropriately.

Instead of a junior person you want to put a very dedicated Senior Product Manager on the job. You need the person who knows the most about the market, the competition and the product to manage the review program and build relationships with the reviewers.

Putting the right person on the job is going to be as important as the product itself. The person has to be somebody who is ultra-responsible, an excellent planner and, ideally, who has run review programs before. It is also important that the person in charge of the program be able to answer tough questions and connect with the reviewers. Many times the way questions are answered will significantly affect what the reviewer chooses to write.

Ultimately, the way the person responsible for the review program treats the reviewer - how responsive they are, what answers they provide, etc. will convey to the reviewer what your company, product and brand are all about.

To get buy-in for putting a senior person in charge of the program you need to convey to your management and executives just how much work and effort the program is going to take. To do this, write a review program plan and present it to the company. The plan should include the goals of the program (how many publications you want to target, how many reviews you want to receive, the number of readers that will be exposed to the reviews, etc.). It should also cover the corresponding tasks & responsibilities, required budget, an overall timeline and required commitments from other departments. If your executives still aren't sure if they want to commit a senior resource find some negative reviews to show them, explaining that you want to avoid having this happen at all costs.

Make sure that the review program responsibilities are written into the quarterly goals of the person running the program so that product reviews are a high priority for them. Have them go on the press tour, meet the reviewers in person, build relationships and follow up and get to know them. Personal relationships go a long way, and if there is a problem the reviewer may be willing to cut you some slack if you have built a good working relationship.

#2: Start Early, Work From a Timeline and Hold Team Meetings

Hold meetings every two weeks once the review program plan is finished (approximately four months prior to the product's ship date), and then once a week once the program has begun. Schedule all activities, deliverables and responsibilities and use a timeline to communicate this to the team and monitor progress. Always factor in at least some amount of schedule slip for the product. For software and hardware products a good rule of thumb is that once you get to Beta you can assume the product will ship one month later than the estimated ship date at that time.

Make sure that the person who is in charge sends status emails after each meeting to the team communicating action items, critical tasks and important issues. Also send a high-level summary to the appropriate executives in the company so that they are aware of the activities and are reassured that the program is proceeding as planned.

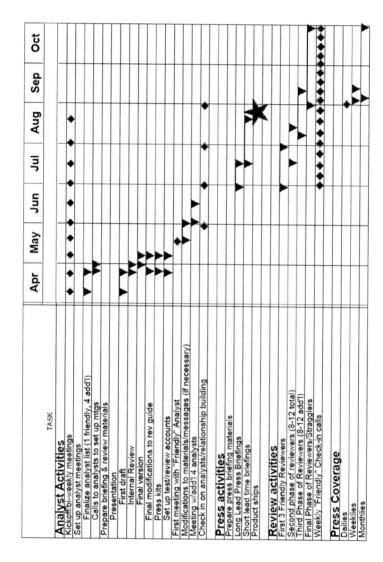

Figure 27: Analyst & Press Program Timeline

In order to get good press coverage, start about four months in advance of the product ship date. This will allow for time to get all of the materials together, such as the messaging, presentation, press kit items, etc. From there, brief the analysts first so that they have formed positive opinions. Following this, brief the longer-lead-time publications such as print magazines so that they can get you on their calendar for coverage several months out. As the launch approaches the shorter-lead-time publications can then be briefed and will be able to contact the analysts for quotes and opinions.

If done correctly the product will ship, you will announce it and you'll receive a flood of coverage initially and then steady ongoing coverage and reviews for the next few months.

#3: Get Your Materials & References Together

It is important to provide a complete set of materials to the reviewer. These should include a press release, brochure, data sheet and a reviewer's guide. Include photos and/or screenshots, and be sure that the screenshots have captions already written on them so the reviewer doesn't have to guess what you are trying highlight. Also include customer quotes, success stories and customer references. And last but not least, include a personalized one-page summary sheet for the reviewer that summarizes all of the materials that are included and gives step-by-step instructions and contact information if they have any problems.

Provide all materials in both printed hard copy and electronic version on a CD in Microsoft Word format. If possible also make the materials available via the Web, ideally in a password-protected manner, in case the reviewer loses the CD or misplaces something. Oftentimes reviewers will use the electronic versions of the documents you provide as the basis for what they write. For example, they may open a document and copy and paste the feature set or other information directly into their article. The goal is to make it very simple for them to write a good review for you, and if you provide materials that they can easily leverage your chances are much better.

Make sure the materials you provide are complete so the reviewer doesn't have to contact you if at all possible. If they have everything they need and can quickly and easily finish the review on their own it will work in your favor. If you provide all of these materials and are well prepared and your competitor doesn't do the same then the reviewer will likely assume that your product is superior and give you a favorable review.

#4: Do the Killer Demo: Practice Practice Practice

Doing a compelling and effective demo of your product during the press tour is critical. It's very possible that this may be the only time when the press actually sees the product. If you have a great demo and credible reference materials and you present your company well, they may not feel the need to actually test the product, and the demo can get you a great review on the spot.

A great demo should highlight the top five features and benefits and appeal to both logic and emotion. Ideally it uses a real-world customer scenario and tells a story. It should build tension, show the top features along the way and then at some point include an unexpected "twist" where the person watching it realizes you're doing something far beyond what they thought would be possible with the product.

Practice your demo with as many people as possible before you go on the press tour. Once you have the demo polished don't change anything. Resist the temptation to sneak in new features (or in the case of a software product to use a newer version of the software). Engineers and executives will always want to add that one little fancy new feature. If you do this and your demo crashes you may not be able to recover your credibility. It is much better to go in with an absolutely solid demo that you know with confidence is going to work 100% of the time.

#5: Make It "Dummy Proof" With Custom Preset Accounts

Make the review process completely "dummy proof." Set up custom, preset demo accounts for each reviewer beforehand and test them several times before the review materials are provided. Be sure that absolutely nothing can go wrong, and then provide the reviewer with the materials and the information for their specific demo account.

If possible, set up the demo so that you can monitor whether they have used the product (by checking whether they have used the license key, logged into the account, etc.). This will provide you with the opportunity to follow up with them to either make sure all is going smoothly if they have used the product or to ask them when they plan to do so and offer additional assistance.

#6: Set the Competitive Argument

It is important that you set the competitive argument for reviewers and to tell them up front who your competitors are. If you don't do this, two things may happen. First, they may put you in a completely different category than you belong in, and compare you with products that are much different from yours and are inappropriate for comparison. Second, you may miss the opportunity to have your product included in product roundup articles where they compare all products in a category.

Tell the press what category you are in, who your main competitors are and why you are superior. Set the competitive argument so that others have to respond to your claims. Provide a competitive matrix and other information to confidently show the reviewer why your product is the winner. Reviewers know that you are going to rig this to make your product look good, but if your competitors haven't done something like this, you will be in a strong position. The reviewer will either have to contact the competitor to clarify the points or they will take your word for it.

	Planet Intra	Hot Office	Intranets.com
Publish and edit web pages without needing to know html?	Yes – using the IntraEditor	No – documents must go through "conversion process"	No
Calendaring, contacts, document posting, and discussion groups?	Yes	Yes	Yes
Structure Intranet to match the way you work?	Yes – by workgroups, teams, departments, or projects	No	No
Hosted & licensed versions available?	Yes	No	No
Administrator can set up and manage all accounts?	Yes	Yes	No – Users must create their own account after being "invited" by admin
"What's New" summary?	Yes	Yes	Yes
Designed to scale up to hundreds of users?	Yes	No – designed for very small teams of 10 or less	No – designed for very small teams of 10 or less
Set security and viewing privileges (read, post, modify) per user or per group?	Yes	No - all users have the ability to view all documents. To keep things confidential you must set up a separate new Intranet.	Yes
Pricing	10 or less users free 11+ users - $6/month/user - volume discounts available	With continuous advertising: Free Without ads: $12.95/month/user for up to 20 users	With continuous advertising: Free

Figure 28: Competitive Comparison Chart

One final point about competition. Don't tell the press that you have no competition. They will find someone to compare you to. If you have a completely unique, breakthrough product then tell them your competition is the "Status Quo" - customers doing things the way they always have because they had no solution like yours.

#7: Phase Rollout, Track Equipment, Check in Routinely

Pick several publications and reviewers early who are as friendly as possible and begin the program with them so that you can iron out the kinks. This will allow you to make sure your license and registration process is working correctly, that the installers work correctly and that any problems with the product are identified and corrected before putting the product into a large number of reviewer's hands.

Don't try to do thirty product reviews all at once. Do the first two or three friendly reviewers, and then roll out a set of eight to ten more. A couple of weeks later roll out the next set of eight to ten, etc. This will ensure that you can stay on top of the review program and be responsive. If you give the product to thirty reviewers at once you may be completely overwhelmed and be unable to respond the reviewers quickly if they have questions or issues.

Track the review program using a simple spreadsheet. If your product is a hardware product, track the date you sent it and the date it is received back. If reviewers have the product for a long period of time this gives you another good reason to contact them to ask what the status of the review is, if there is anything they need and also to let them know you need the review unit back to provide to the next reviewer.

Keep in contact with the reviewers on a routine basis to make sure everything is going smoothly. Call them two days after the product and reviewer's kit has been sent to them just to check in and make sure they received everything and are aware of all of the materials you have provided. Following this, make a friendly call every week or so to make sure things are going smoothly. This will ensure that if anything has gone wrong during the review process you have the best possible chance of responding and remedying the situation.

#8: Provide Immediate Responses

Always provide immediate responses to reviewers. Once a reviewer begins to review your product the last thing you want to have happen is for them to have to wait for a response from you, stall their efforts and lose momentum.

If at all possible, provide instantaneous responses to any questions that reviewers have. In the worst case, respond within two hours. If a call or email comes in, drop everything else and get them an answer. Give them the cell phone number of the person responsible for the program so that they can reach them immediately. And get commitment from product management, engineering, support and anyone else about providing this type of response time.

Providing immediate responses is absolutely critical because it is essentially the parachute if the reviewer actually trips and falls out of the plane. If something goes wrong but you provide an immediate response the reviewer may still view your company and product favorably and choose to not include the details in the review. However, if you are not responsive they may decide to write a scathing review and indicate that they can't recommend your product.

#9: Include Screenshots & Photos With Captions

Be sure to include screenshots and photos with captions. Include images that represent a variety so that reviewers and editors can choose from the different ones and don't feel that they're going to run the same photo or screenshots as other publications.

Screenshots should highlight the top three features of your product and include captions that are visible when the graphic is opened. Oftentimes, reviewers will use the caption you include as a direct quote and put it right in the review (particularly if they are on deadline).

Many times publications will take their own screenshots. Having several good examples showing them what is important gives them an idea of what to highlight and what to say, and they are likely to leverage what you have provided. This is another example of making it as easy as possible for the reviewer. By providing everything they need, you load the deck in favor of getting a great review for your product.

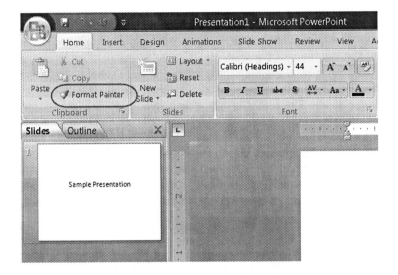

"With the Format Painter tool you can copy formatting from one section of text to another quickly and easily"

Figure 29: Screen Shot with Caption

Here's an example of a sample screenshot; we actually circled the most important portion and put the caption down at the bottom so there is no doubt about what is important.

#10: Write the Review for Them

The number one way to get a great review is provide a comprehensive and thorough reviewer's guide. In doing so you significantly reduce the amount of work the reviewer needs to do because you have already done it for them.

The reviewer's guide should include an overview and introduction that sets the stage in terms of what is important when reviewing this type of product and what is important to the customer. It should include a guided tour that takes them through the product feature by feature, showing them the top five to seven features using screenshots and captions that walk them through. And it may also include information about what's coming in the future (particularly important if your product is weak in one area versus its competitors and you want the reviewer to mention that you will be providing the functionality in the near future). Also include competitive information and a summary and contact information. Note: there is a reviewer's guide template included in the Product Review Program Toolkit, available at www.280group.com in the "Products Section."

One of the most important things to include is a FAQ (frequently asked questions) section. If the reviewer has one place where they go to double-check the pricing, product details, ship date, warranties, support policies, etc., it can reduce their need to call or email you.

Sample Reviewer's Guide Outline

I.   Overview
II.   Introduction
III. What to consider when evaluating solutions
IV.   Guided tour
V.   Coming Soon...
VI.   Summary
VII. Contact Information
VIII. Competitive Comparison
IX.   FAQ: Frequently Asked Questions

Figure 30: Reviewer's Guide Outline

If possible use a graphic designer to lay out the guide and provide professionally-printed copies to all reviewers. This can be an expensive endeavor but it can also be worth every penny because it creates a positive impression and further increases your company's credibility. It's possible that a reviewer will evaluate your product based solely on the reviewer's guide without ever setting up or using the product. If they can get a quick idea of what the product does and what features are important and you have established credibility through your demo and materials they may not feel the need to spend time using the product.

As mentioned before, make sure you provide Adobe Acrobat PDF and Microsoft Word versions of the reviewer's guide. You want the reviewers to plagiarize as much as possible. Put words in their mouth if you possibly can. Ideally they'll just simply copy much of the text, such as the feature list, change the wording and put it directly in the review.

Reviewer's guides are also very useful for a variety of other purposes, such as training your sales force and channels as well as familiarizing the other groups in your company with the product's capabilities. And if you have a thorough FAQ section you can point people to it for common questions to reduce the amount of time you spend answering the same questions over and over again.

6 Conclusion

In this book we have covered four of the most critical aspects for product success: roadmapping and planning, beta programs, product launches and product review programs. Our hope is that the tips, strategies and techniques presented here will help you and other readers to bring some excellent new products to market, beat your competition and achieve success.

We would love to hear from you if you have additional tips, comments or suggestions regarding what has worked for you in defining, launching and marketing your products, or if you have ideas for additional templates and toolkits that you would like to see us bring to market. Feel free to email us your ideas at expertpm@280group.com.

Product Management Resources

The 280 Group website is constantly updated with the latest Product Management and Product Marketing Resources including:

- Free templates, samples & white papers

- Product Management Blogs

- Product Management & Product Marketing Books

- Product Management Associations

- Product Management Software Comparison

Visit www.280group.com and check the "Resources" section for the most up-to-date listings.

Also, be sure to subscribe to our free Product Management 2.0 newsletter at www.280group.com/newsletters.htm and via RSS to our "Product Management 2.0" Blog located at www.280group.com/blog.html.

B | Templates

The 280 Group also offers Product Management & Product Marketing Toolkits, which include templates, narrated training presentations and samples. The toolkits can be purchased at www.280group.com. The examples in this book and the methodology presented use the templates in the Toolkits, which cover the following topics:

- Product Roadmap Toolkit™

- Product Launch Toolkit™

- Product Manager's Toolkit™

- Beta Program Toolkit™

- Product Review Program Toolkit™

- Developer Program Toolkit™

The toolkits are also available as part of the 280 Group PM Office™. The PM Office Professional version includes all six toolkits, and the Standard version includes the Roadmap, Launch and Product Manager's Toolkits.

NOTE By purchasing this book you are entitled to a $30 discount on the PM Office Professional version. To take advantage of this offer go to the PM Office in the "Products" section of the 280 Group website at www.280group.com. When you place your order for the PM Office Professional go to the bottom of the page, enter the promo code "337844", click submit and then proceed with your purchase. Note: the $30 discount applies only at the time of purchase and may not be redeemed at a later date.

The 280 Group also makes a number of templates available free for download on the 280 Group website at www.280group.com in the "Resources" section under "Free PM Tools," including the following:

- MRD Outline

- Feature Prioritization Matrix

- Beta Program Bug & Feature Database Tools

- Adwords ROI calculator

- Sample Product Roadmaps

- Developer Program Roadmap

- Developer Program Cost Estimator Tool

- Evangelism Timeline

- Competitive Feature Matrix Comparison Chart

- Product Launch Plan Marketing Budget

- Press Release

- Google AdWords Tips & Strategies

We are constantly adding new free templates and toolkits, so check back often.

About the Author

Brian Lawley is the President and Founder of the 280 Group, a Product Management services firm that provides consulting, contractors, training and templates. He is also President of the Silicon Valley Product Management Association, the world's largest Product Management Association. During his twenty year career in Product Management he has defined, launched and marketed over fifty successful products for companies such as Apple, Symantec, Adobe, Palm and dozens of startup and mid-sized companies.

Mr. Lawley was nominated for the Product Management Excellence Award for Thought Leadership by the Association of International Product Marketing & Management in 2006 and 2007. He is the editor of Product Management 2.0, a newsletter and Blog devoted to excellence in Product Management and routinely writes guest articles for a variety of other publications. He frequently speaks on the topic of Product Management, has delivered several keynote addresses at well-known conferences and has been featured on CNBC's World Business Review and the Silicon Valley Business Report.

Mr. Lawley is a Certified Product Manager (CPM) and Certified Product Marketing Manager (CPMM). He earned an MBA with honors from San Jose State University and a Bachelors Degree in Management Science from the University of California at San Diego with a Minor in Music Technology.

Create Thought Leadership for your Company

Books deliver instant credibility to the author. Having an MBA or PhD is great, however, putting the word "author" in front of your name is similar to using the letters PHD or MBA. You are no long Michael Green, you are "Author Michael Green."

Books give you a platform to stand on. They help you to:

- Demonstrate your thought leadership
- Generate leads

Books deliver increased revenue, particularly indirect revenue

- A typical consultant will make 3x in indirect revenue for every dollar they make on book sales

Books are better than a business card. They are:

- More powerful than white papers
- An item that makes it to the book shelf vs. the circular file
- The best tschocke you can give at a conference

Why wait to write your book?

Check out other companies that have built credibility by writing and publishing a book through Happy About

Contact Happy About at 408-257-3000 or go to http://happyabout.info.

Other Happy About Books

Projects are MESSY!

From the minute the project begins, all manner of changes, surprises and disasters befall them. Unfortunately most of these are PREDICTABLE and AVOIDABLE.

Paperback $19.95
eBook $11.95

Learn the 42 Rules of Marketing!

Compilation of ideas, theories, and practical approaches to marketing challenges that marketers know they should do, but don't always have the time or patience to do.

Paperback $19.95
eBook $11.95

Books

Printed in the United States
116867LV00003BA/103-201/A